# PHILADELPHIA
## *IN COLOR*

*Profiles of America*

# PHILADELPHIA
## *in Color*

*Introductory Text
and Notes on the Illustrations by*
*JOHN P. HAYES*
*With a Collection of Color*
*Photographs by*
RAYMOND A. NOLL AND ROGER TAUSS

HASTINGS HOUSE · PUBLISHERS
*New York, 10016*

## ACKNOWLEDGEMENTS

Whenever two or more Philadelphians get together to discuss the city or their neighborhoods, there is always the risk that they'll rekindle the American Revolution *and* the Civil War. Fortunately, Charles and Diana Kleaver (from Kensington and South Philly, respectively) and Ed and Dotty Clark (from Mayfair and Tacony, respectively) restrained themselves through deadline, and for their contributions the author is grateful. Appreciation is also extended to Samuel B. Rogers of the Philadelphia Convention and Visitors Bureau, and to the research staff of the Philadelphia Free Library.

PUBLISHED 1983 BY HASTINGS HOUSE, PUBLISHERS, INC.

*Reprinted March, 1988*

Library of Congress Cataloging in Publication Data

Hayes, John Phillip, 1949-
  Philadelphia in color.

  (Profiles of America)
  1. Philadelphia (Pa.)—Description—1981-
2. Philadelphia (Pa.)—History. I. Noll, Raymond A.
II. Tauss, Roger. III. Title. IV. Series.
F158.52.H38 1983 974.8'1104  82-23391
ISBN 0-8038-5898-1

*Printed and bound in Hong Kong by Mandarin Offset*
Distributed to the trade by:
Kampmann & Co., Inc., New York, NY

# CONTENTS

# THE BIG LITTLE TOWN

I F America's Bicentennial Committee had intended the nation's 200th birthday party to last just one year, no one informed Philadelphia, and in this city the party continues. The Bicentennial inspired a cultural renaissance that promises not to die in the City of Brotherly Love, and now, even Philadelphians, the very people who traditionally poke fun at their town, are inviting friends to "Come and get it, Philadelphia style."

No other city—not zany New York, not proud Boston, not merry San Francisco, not shiny Houston—offers Americans a style more meaningful than Philadelphia's. Here, style equates friendship and freedom.

Nearly five million people from all corners of the world contribute to Philadelphia's style, and no matter who they are, what they do, or how much they earn, most of them seek one common goal: to live in, or near, a big little town. They have found it in Philadephia, the country's fourth most populous city, and, according to *Places Rated Almanac*, the sixth best place to live in America. In spite of Philadelphia's size, says the FBI, it is one of the safest cities in the nation.

Philadelphia vibrates because of its people. Artists and athletes. Lawyers and stockbrokers. Doctors and scientists. Professors and museum curators. Businessmen and women. Street vendors and merchants. Among these professions are dozens more, all of them lending to the hustle and bustle of Philadelphia's streets.

Some people love the busy pace of Philadelphia. They race from the Broad Street subway to City Hall, past the Clothespin sculpture and through the turnstiles of tall office buildings, and then run to the newsstands for their *Daily News* and a soft pretzel smeared with mustard. Later, they join the shopping lines at John Wanamaker and catch their breath over dinner in Chinatown before the Phillies game at the Vet.

Equally as many other Philadelphians have nowhere to go in a hurry. (Some, the bag ladies and street bums have nowhere to go, ever.) Thousands of Philadelphians are small-town folks, many of them transplants from the Midwest.

They savor the East Coast's best-kept secret in slow gear. They mosey through the Philadelphia Museum of Art, one of the world's finest; they shop along Antiques' Row and sample ethnic foods on South Street. They admire the Liberty Bell, stroll along Penn's Landing, and eat Philadelphia's famous ice cream on park benches from where they watch the city pass by.

Ah, it's a glorious town, Philadelphia, constantly changing, ever-mindful of its future, and haunted by 300 years of history — the nation's most dramatic and colorful history. Almost everything once happened here, or was invented here, so no city in America offers more surprises than Philadelphia. Yes, there are problems. Unemployment is high; good, moderate-priced housing is scarce; the educational system appears ready to collapse; racism frequently raises its ugly head; a burdensome bureaucracy slows political and social progress; cabs are impossible to hail; the weather is unpredictable; and safety worries residents in certain neighborhoods. But every metropolis has problems. None, however, boasts the style of Philadelphia, a gift unique to its people. A gift bestowed upon the city at birth.


## William Penn and His "Holy Experiment"

From William Penn's likeness on a popular, round box of cereal sold in American supermarkets today, we could assume that Philadelphia's founding father was a happy, fat-faced Quaker with ne'er a worry in the world. Untrue to history, Penn's image has been distorted on that box of cereal. For Penn's life was marred by debt, personal tragedies and depression, particularly after he settled Philadelphia, his refuge from persecution, his "Holy Experiment," his promised land.

For Penn, life began in England where his father, Admiral Sir William Penn, expected him to attend Oxford and aspire to a seat of honor in the court of England. Handsome and rebellious, he did enroll at Oxford but he refused to attend chapel. Expelled, he appeased his disappointed family by studying theology, then law, and in his twenties, well-educated and socially aware, he managed his family's estate in Ireland.

One day Penn heard the Quaker itinerant Thomas Loe preach, "There is a Faith that overcomes the World, and there is a Faith that is overcome by the World." Immediately he became a convinced Quaker, committing himself and his social status to the Society of Friends, a radical religious sect repeatedly persecuted in England for its dissenting views. Such defiance shocked Penn's family and friends, most of whom shunned him while he was imprisoned on four occasions. But in spite of them, and prison life, he persevered. Soon Penn realized that if he planned to preach and write freely as a Quaker, he would have to flee his homeland and people and seek tolerance on another continent. This, then, led him to become a religious leader, a social philosopher, and a colonial proprietor.

Members of the Society of Friends encouraged Penn as he applied his energy towards religious, political and intellectual freedom. Eventually their needs, coupled with his, led him to petition the Crown for a grant of land in the New World, where *all* men and women could practice their beliefs and live peacefully.

To satisfy a considerable debt owed by the duke of York to Penn's deceased father, the duke's brother, King Charles II, granted William Penn 26,000,000 acres in America. "I believe," Penn accurately predicted after he accepted the charter on March 14, 1681, "my God that has given it me, through many difficulties, will bless and make it the seed of a nation."

This land in the New World became Penn's "Holy Experiment," his refuge for Quakers and all others who hoped to begin life anew, share freedom of mind and spirit, and escape perscution, war and famine. Of course, this land became even greater.

Penn's charter made him Lord Proprietor of a vast wilderness, the south-eastern tip of which connected the eleven existing colonies in America. Thus, we call Pennsylvania the Keystone State. In two lush, square miles of that tip, Penn decided to build a town. He chose his site carefully, ensuring the town's future economic importance. The two square miles contained dry, fertile land, bound by two rivers teeming with fish, the Delaware River flowing east and south, and the Schuylkill (School Kill) River flowing from the northwest. The confluence of the rivers, south of Penn's property, provided waterfront access to the precious farmland and inland resources lying beyond the town, which Penn envisioned as a major port. Furthermore, colonial travelers frequently had to pass through Penn's land, and the horse and carriage society would be drawn to his town as a convenient meeting place. Here then, on a site affording prominence and growth, Penn elected to raise Philadelphia, a name he derived from two Greek words, *philia* and *adelphas*, together meaning Brotherly Love.

Already, Lenni-Lenape Indians, the "original people," lived along the Delaware River, and some pioneering Swedes had settled in the area about 1636, naming their village Wicaco (meaning "pleasant place"). Penn deplored the crowded, depressing conditions of the masses in his native London, so before sailing from England he instructed his surveyor general, Thomas Holme, to lay out the town in a spacious gridiron pattern of streets with five squares, allowing large plots for the residents. He directed his cousin, William Markham, as deputy governor, to "let every house be pitched in the middle of its plot so that there may be ground on each side for gardens and orchards or fields, that it may be a greene countrie towne that will never be burnt and always be wholesome."

When Markham and Holme arrived in America they surveyed the five parks, one in the center of town and the other four connected diagonally from the center. They laid out a gridiron street pattern beginning at Front Street near the Delaware River, eventually extending it westward across 26 blocks to the Schuylkill River. They named the town's southern boundary Cedar Street, now South Street, and the northern boundary, thirteen blocks away, Vine Street. (Today, we call this area center city.)

Numbered streets ran north and south, with the lowest numbers closest to the Delaware River, and streets named for shrubs and trees ran east and west. Two major roads, both 100 feet wide, twice the width of most other streets, intersected at the center square, now the site of City Hall. The busiest of the two was High Street, now Market Street, running across town for twelve miles. It crossed Broad Street, one of the ten north-south arteries not to be numbered.

Along with Philadelphia's physical layout, Penn also provided Markham and Holme with the town's liberal frame of government. He wanted power to remain with the governor and his council—a clause that eventually irritated many Quakers—but free men retained the right to alter the system if they so desired. Among other privileges, Penn also guaranteed liberty of conscience, the right for taxpayers to vote, and a trial by jury.

With these plans in motion, Penn advertised the "Holy Experiment" in England, Holland and Germany. To entice settlers he offered clear title to a building lot in the town, an 80-acre farm on the outskirts, and 5,000 acres in the hinterlands, all for a cost of about $1,000. There were smaller, economy packages, too. This was the promised land, Penn said in his advertisements, full of animal life, streams filled with fish, great flocks of passenger pigeons, orchards, flowers, and all of it "sweet from the Cedar, Pine and Sassafras." Penn's notice, which was not an exaggeration of his property, attracted even the least adventurous men and women, and droves of people from all parts of Europe hired passage across the Atlantic. From the outset, Penn's town would be ethnically diverse, a refuge for people from all walks of life, the poor, the craftsmen, the intellectuals, and many of them well-to-do.

In the fall of 1682, Penn prepared for his own passage to the New World but regretfully without his ailing wife and four children. One hundred Quakers accompanied him to America on a 300-ton bark, which for eight weeks battled gales all the way over. Thirty of the Quakers died of smallpox and were buried at sea.

Upon arrival at Philadelphia, Penn supposedly leaped ashore, weary but healthy, and danced in celebration with the Indians. That night, legend holds, he slept in the Blue Anchor tavern near Dock Creek, not far from the river, and the principal landmark on the shore.

When Penn arrived, construction of Philadelphia's squares and streets was near completion, and there were 18 small brick houses standing and many more underway. Settlers continued arriving — Penn reported to London in late 1682 that 22 ships had docked since his *Welcome* — but people lived in caves along the river banks until housing became available. Soon there were more settlers than plots of land within Philadelphia proper, and Penn provided land in the Northern Liberties immediately north of the town along the Delaware.

In almost every direction beyond Philadelphia the wilderness seemed endless. Slowly the settlers cleared their properties, built their dwellings, opened a marketplace and shops, and in time the peninsula between the Delaware and Schuylkill Rivers began to satisfy Penn's expectations. Swedes, Dutch, Germans and English arrived in the late 1600's, followed by more English in the 1700's, Irish and more Germans in the mid-1800's, Italians, Eastern European Jews, Poles and Slavs through the 1920's and Spanish-speaking people and blacks several decades later. Blacks were also in Philadelphia during Penn's time, some of them, incredible as it sounds, slaves at Quaker Penn's country mansion.

Because each group of settlers brought to America new ideas and a variety of religious practices, Philadelphia soon had churches of all denominations. For some years the Quakers remained the religious and political ruling class, but their dominance waned as other sects arrived. By the turn of the century, German Mennonites, Lutherans, Scotch-Irish Presbyterians, Welsh Baptists, Catholics and even a Church of England party practiced their faiths in Penn's expanding town.

Of course this mixture of people and lifestyles rounded out Penn's plan, and the harmony of his community marked the success of the "Holy Experiment." For two years Penn "presided like a handsome deity over his growing colony, which for a little while was the elysium he thought it," according to Struthers Burt in *Philadelphia: Holy Experiment*. "He was immensely pleased with everything."

At the end of two years, however, a boundary dispute between the Crown and the colonies forced Penn's reluctant return to London. With his dusty town laid out, his government established, and $100,000 profit earned from his enterprise, the Lord Proprietor promised not to be gone long. He stayed away for fifteen years!

The independence of the colonies depended upon Penn's influence. When William and Mary dethroned James II, Penn fell into grave disfavor, and for two years he lost control of Pennsylvania. Later, he managed to re-assemble his political alliances and return to America in 1699 as a spokeman for independence. With him arrived his second wife, Hannah Callowhill, two surviving children from his first marriage, and his personal secretary and confidential agent, James Logan, who became a distinguished Philadelphian. Imagine the excitement Penn must have felt seeing his town again from the sea. He had left it a small, red brick village along the river banks, with about 300 houses, but Philadephia had more than doubled in size while he was away. Unfortunately the town was really no longer his.

The welcoming party was less than gracious, and except for the Indians and a few older Quakers, people were polite, but cold. Penn had been away too long. His "Holy Experiment" had been reduced to an ideal of the past, a once successful, but now almost meaningless exercise in the minds of many people who seemed to have forgotten that tolerance had guided them to this New World.

Ironically, Penn's arrival coincided with a war brewing between the churches, and in the middle of the controversy were Penn's own quiet Friends. The Quakers, it appeared, argued with everyone, including Penn. In their quest for legislative power, the Quakers debated Penn's political system of government and resented his role as absentee landlord. Other sects shared similar feelings about Penn, but they also repudiated the Quakers for their pacifism, their ascendancy, and for what Struthers Burt called "their quiet, not un-smug, theory of tolerance." Members of the Church of England, who were generally among the upper crust of Philadelphia's society, and whom the Quakers, without Penn's knowledge, originally denied a parish, were always at odds with the Quakers, and they threatened to capture control of Penn's province and return it to the Crown.

Penn felt reluctant to mix politics with his "Holy Experiment," or perhaps he was not a politician after all. At home in the New World of tolerance, where people were becoming less tolerant, he permitted himself to relax. He tried keeping the peace for two years, but his presence annoyed most residents.

All but Penn's friends and admirers objected to his lavish lifestyle. He lived grandly in both town and country, enjoying the Slate Roof House built for him on Second Street, and a mansion at Pennsbury on the Delaware. The country dwelling was magnificent, costing Penn five thousand pounds. A brick home and outbuildings, including stables, sat among lawns and gardens with trees and flowers transported from the other colonies and imported from England. Five English gardeners tended the property. Servants and slaves, most of them black, cared for the home and worked the farm. They also served the guests whom Penn loved to entertain, offering them a variety of expensive food, some of it imported, and the best of wines from Europe. Penn dressed fashionably, too, being fussy about his wigs and hose and usually favoring a bright blue sash. He spent much of his time visiting people, including the Indians who called him the "white truth teller," and when he traveled from country to town, he either floated down the Delaware in a twelve-oared barge, or bounced along rutted roads in a four-horse coach.

He listened patiently to people's problems and gave away large sums of money, even though he was often himself in debt. But his extravagance and vanity offended most Quakers and many others, too, until they considered him a nuisance. Penn and his emissaries were continuously rebuffed by the Quaker-dominated Assembly in Philadelphia, and even after he granted the Assembly pre-eminence in the Charter of Privileges, the Lord Proprietor remained un-popular.

Pained but not resigned to give up the "Holy Experiment," Penn lived in America until 1701 when yet another dispute demanded his attention in England. In October, he and his party, including his wife and Logan, left Pennsbury and sailed for Portsmouth. Penn said this time he would return without delay, a promise that mattered to few people, but he would never return.

He attempted to rule the "Holy Experiment" from abroad, but proved ineffective. Soon he felt discouraged. His personal steward defrauded him of thousands of pounds, and the Assembly continued to disregard his ideas.

In 1702, Logan advised Penn to sell the "Holy Experiment," and by 1712 Penn negotiated but never consummated a sale. A stroke left the Lord Proprietor seriously ill that year. Throughout the duration of his illness the words "Holy Experiment" intensified his depression. He died six years later, having spent only four years in the land that he had envisioned as the "seed of a nation." Philadelphia, and Pennsylvania, passed to his wife, Hannah, who never liked the New World. Proprietorship remained with the Penn family until the American Revolution.


# Philadelphia's Golden Era

Thirty-six years after Philadelphia's birth, William Penn's death knell sounded across the Atlantic, but life never missed a beat in the City of Brotherly Love. Upon word of the founding father's death, there occurred a respectful pause within the community, but Penn, and his "Holy Experiment," were now of little interest. Men of equal and even greater talent, men of noble ideas and fantastic imaginations, began settling in the city, creating for Philadelphia a Golden Era. Penn died on the eve of this exciting age, the years between 1720 and 1800, when

Philadelphia evolved as the social, intellectual, artistic, scientific and political hub of the colonies.

The first man to dominate the city was Benjamin Franklin, Philadelphia's Godfather. He arrived in 1723, penniless and shabby, a rebel from Boston where he had been an unhappy printer's apprentice. After a brief stay in New York, Franklin drifted into Philadephia, a handsome boy of 17 with less than two years formal education. He established himself as a printer, won many friends, and through various interests provided much of the stimulation that marked Philadelphia's Golden Era. An almost endless list of credits and "firsts" belong to Benjamin Franklin. A few of his most important achievements are these:

He experimented with electricity, shock treatment and electric cooking. (Supposedly he electrocuted a turkey along the banks of the Schuylkill in 1749, then roasted the bird electrically for a picnic with several astonished friends). He organized the Junto in 1727, a discussion club from which came the Library Company of Philadephia, the first circulating library in America, and the American Philosophical Society; he established a fire fighting company, a fire insurance company, a charitable school, which later became the University of Pennsylvania, and the Pennsylvania Hospital, America's first charity hospital; he created the country's postal system, served as postmaster, published a newspaper, and late in his life made the first pair of bifocals.

Talent, persistence and wit led Benjamin Franklin to the forefront of Philadelphia society, but he was not always the city's beloved son. Franklin *was* an agitator, "always improving, petitioning, scolding, upsetting," wrote Struthers Burt, "a . . . most annoying and disturbing citizen to those who believe in the status quo."

As an astute politician, Franklin had a sly way of setting progress in motion. He won support for lighted streets and other civic improvements in the city. He was Philadelphia's most illustrious civic leader and 18th century America's most creative citizen. Even in old age he crossed the Atlantic to negotiate peace. At all times, Benjamin Franklin remained a calming force in a revolutionary town.

During Franklin's life in Philadelphia, quiet turned to turbulence and then, to war. There were about 10,000 residents within the city's boundaries in 1720, and 23,700 residents at the time of the American Revolution, but there were many more people living in the ethnic neighborhoods bordering the city. Each neighborhood offered a distinct, comfortable lifestyle, but no matter where people lived, their attention always centered on Philadelphia. Most activities occurred in the vicinity of east High Street around the traditional English open-air markets that offered fresh produce from New Jersey, just across the Delaware. Along the street and in the alleys, small shops representing 71 different occupations —

14

including silversmiths, printers, goldsmiths, artisans, braziers, pewterers, dyers, combmakers, chaisemakers, a breechesmaker, hatters and stocking weavers — served the patrons who bartered and haggled for their goods. The sidewalks were crowded and noisy, with street criers singing out their wares: Pepper Pot ... Hot Corn ... Soft Soap ... Charcoal. The post office and the original city hall were in this part of town, too, and nearby was Christ Church, the first Anglican Church in America where worshippers included many soon-to-be famous Americans.

Historians have said that from a ship on the Delaware looking inland, Philadelphia resembled London without steeples, and indeed the city grew second only to London in numbers of English-speaking population. Philadelphia became one of the British empire's most important business centers, out-produced only by Liverpool and London. "Everybody in Philadelphia deals more or less in trade," noted a visitor in 1756. The colonists maintained a triangular trade relationship with the West Indies and England. In exchange for lumber, furs, wheat and flour the West Indies traded sugar, rum and molasses which the colonists, along with locally produced bar iron and wheat, then exported to England for manufactured goods. Complementing the colonists' trade activities were several thriving professions. Banking, insurance and law contributed a spirit of progress throughout Philadelphia.

Romanticizing this era requires little imagination. On any given day walking down the street, passersby might have see Benjamin Rush, the great physician, David Rittenhouse, an early aristocrat and astronomer, Charles Willson Peale, the artist, Francis Hopkinson, lawyer and poet, Isaac Norris, merchant and member of the Pennsylvania Assembly, Andrew Hamilton, famous attorney, and Clement Biddle, merchant and importer.

Life was serious then, and full of troubles and hardships, among them deathly illnesses, unsanitary conditions, crime and piracy. Duels flourished in the 1700's and drunken brawls, some committed by William Penn, II !, forced watchmen to patrol the city after nightfall. One visitor reported that "no place was more overcome with wickedness, sins so scandalous, openly committed, in defiance of law and virtue." Even so, a police force was not formed until 1854.

Most of the city's residents had fun without breaking the law, but Quakers seemed to have the least fun of all. Thompson Westcott wrote in his *History of Philadelphia* that Friends had but two recourses against ennui: going to meeting and enjoying the pleasures of the table, thus contributing to the town's eventual nickname, "The City of Homes."

Reading, skating, swimming and fishing were other wholesome activities approved by the Quakers. Of these, fishing in the Schuylkill seemed to be a favorite. A well known fisherman reported catching 3,000 catfish in the Schuylkill waters one night, but he may have told America's first fish story.

"Evil sports and games" were taboo for the Quakers because such events encouraged gambling and betting. Even so, the colonists raced horses along Sassafras Street, now Race Street, where without doubt they also did some wagering! Cock fights were popular, as were boxing matches, billiards, card playing and quoits. Many of the refined colonists preferred concerts, dances, museum tours and the theatre, and these pleasantries became so popular that by the time of the Revolution, people considered Philadelphia the "Athens of America."

Not all Philadelphians cared much about politics — although in later years it has been noted that at bedtime mothers instructed their children to pray for the Pennsylvania Railroad, the Girard Trust, and the Republican Party. Throughout the 18th century, Pennsylvania's lawmakers met in Philadelphia, as did members of the Supreme Court, and from 1790 to 1800, the new federal government met here. So there was always a meeting in session, or some proclamation about to be announced.

Originally Pennsylvania's legislative Assembly, with members elected from all parts of the province, met in private homes in Philadephia, but in 1729 a committee devised plans for a State House to be located between Fifth and Sixth Streets, on Chestnut Street. Andrew Hamilton selected the building site, work-men cleared it of whortleberry bushes and peach trees, and sent several cows elsewhere to graze. Master Carpenter Edmund Woolley began construction in 1732, the year of George Washington's birth.

Inexperienced laborers and a shortage of money slowed progress, but in 1735, while construction continued, the impatient legislators moved into a two-story, unadorned red brick building. With the east and west wings completed during the next year, the State House stretched the entire length of the block. Inside on the first floor of the main building a central hallway divided two spacious meeting rooms — one for the Assembly, the other for the Supreme Court — and upstairs were meeting rooms, office space, and a long dining room stretching across the front of the building.

After many years in session the Assembly decided to dress up the State House with a tower and belfry. Then the building became the showplace of the colonies. Isaac Norris, Speaker of the House, wrote to London in 1751 to order a bell of "about two thousand pounds weight" to be inscribed with the Old Testament phrase, "Proclaim Liberty throughout all the land unto all the inhabitants thereof." Remember, this was 1751, a quarter of a century prior to the Revolution. No one then could have possibly imagined the significance of that inscription, or the symbolism of the bell itself to future American generations.

Delivery of the bell to the docks of Philadephia probably attracted a crowd, and everyone must have sighed when the bell's clapper struck for the first time and cracked the shell! Two foundrymen required nearly a year to recast the bell twice to achieve a solid tone, and then in June, 1753, workmen hung the bell in the State House tower. Protected by its white cupola, the bell added elegance to an otherwise ordinary looking building. For 80 years, except for several months of interruption during the Revolution, the bell tolled the hour and announced special events in Philadelphia, but then the bell cracked a second time, now beyond repair. Thereafter, the bell, by this time called the Liberty Bell, has hung in silence.

In the early 1770's, a nation was uniting here, slowly, sometimes unwillingly. In the fall of 1774, twelve colonies sent 56 delegates to Philadelphia to convene the First Continental Congress. The representatives included George Washington, John Adams, Samuel Adams, Richard Henry Lee, Patrick Henry, and Peyton Randolph, who was elected president. They accepted the challenge of resolving the colonies' political differences with the Mother Country, and for seven weeks they met in a chilly Carpenters' Hall, not far from the State House. War was never a serious consideration in their deliberations. These loyal Englishmen, moderate in tone for the most part, believed they could legislate both peace *and* freedom, and to accomplish their goal they respectfully petitioned King George III to repeal all regulatory acts since 1763 — the Intolerable Acts being most offensive. As a measure of their sincerity the delegates restricted trade with England, and as a precaution, they advised each of the colonies to organize and train a militia. However, few of the representatives doubted the good King's intentions. He would grant relief, they said. But before going home they agreed to meet again in May, just in case the King surprised them. After adjournment, the delegates affirmed their loyalty at a grand banquet, raising the first toast "To His Majesty King George III, our Royal Sovereign." There seemed hardly a strain in the town, for when John Adams wrote to his wife, as he often did, he used the words, "happy, elegant, tranquil, and polite," to describe Philadelphia society.

Within months, shots at Lexington and Concord convinced many of the colonists that King George had answered. Instead of relief, the King sent Redcoats. Now war was inevitable. The Second Continental Congress convened on May 10, 1775. This time, the delegates met in the State House, soon to be known as Independence Hall. Many of them insisted on sending a second petition to the King, hopeful for a peaceful settlement, but radical members of Congress also pushed for the formation of an army, and in June, George Washington became commander-in-chief. That same month, the bloody Battle of Bunker Hill justified the most loyal Englishman's cry for revolution.

Benjamin Franklin, now 70, just back from a nine year mission in Europe, joined those who sought mutual reconciliation. The British, with Europe's best professional soldiers, would overpower a nation so young, so inexperienced and without resources for war. But Bunker Hill and other battles changed Franklin's mind, and once he supported independence, he helped sway Pennsylvania's Assembly. "They that can give up essential liberty to obtain a little temporary safety deserve neither liberty nor safety," warned the wise old gentleman.

On June 7, Richard Henry Lee of Virginia spoke the now famous words, "That these United Colonies are, and of right ought to be, free and independent States . . . ." To satisfy that resolution, Congress assigned a committee to write a declaration of independence. Franklin, John Adams, Robert Sherman, Robert Livingston and Thomas Jefferson served on the committee, but Jefferson, age 33, actually wrote the document. This earthy, red-haired Virginian, who played the violin and liked to work alone, cornered himself on the second floor of the Graff House at Seventh and Market Streets and wrote the first draft before the end of June. With little editing, the committee presented the declaration to Congress. An observer that July, peeking through the State House windows, which along with the doors remained closed to keep out pesky flies from a nearby stable, could have watched the members argue for two days about the document's contents. Jefferson, his head bowed, his work completed, never said a word, but Adams, quick and eloquent, debated every last syllable. Late in the evening of a muggy July 4, the room now sweltering, the Congress accepted the document. No speeches, no celebrations followed the vote. Everyone felt too exhausted for that, and too worried.

Meanwhile, to fight a war a country had to show its colors, and to that end George Washington and two others supposedly visited the widow Betsy Ross and asked her to sew a flag. Historians continue to disagree about who actually made the first flag — Francis Hopkinson claimed he did — but legend says that young Mrs. Ross, who ran an upholstery shop from her home on Arch Street, made a striped, red and white flag with thirteen five-pointed stars, white in a blue field "representing a new constellation." She then presented the flag to Washington, whose troops carried it into battle.

Not everyone in Philadephia felt as patriotic as Betsy Ross or as confident as George Washington, and even after Congress had declared independence and the colonies were several months at war, at least 3,000 Philadephians remained loyal to England. It must have been a glorious sight for these loyalists when Lord Charles Cornwallis and Sir William General Howe marched 18,000 redcoats into the city in 1777, dragging behind them 500 prisoners and scattering the

Continental Congress and most patriots into the country. General William Maxwell had tried unsuccessfully to stop the British advance at Cooch's Bridge in Delaware, where the Stars and Stripes first fluttered in war. Later, General Washington's troops planned to rout the enemy, fighting at nearby Germantown from where the cannon fire rattled the State House windows, but the mighty British turned the General and his men towards Valley Forge, and that ugly, depressing winter of 1777–78.

The loyalists remained at home to aid the British, who turned the first floor of the State House into the Provost Marshall's headquarters, and the second floor into a jail. Fortunately, the Liberty Bell, with its fiery inscription so bold and intent, had already been removed for safekeeping, the Americans fearing the British would melt it for ammunition.

How crude seemed the British soldiers in the City of Brotherly Love. How reckless these polished intruders. They dug a hole in the State House yard and filled it with dead horses and human bodies. They mistreated their prisoners, depriving them of food for days at a time. Of course they befriended the townsfolk, wooed the women, and most evenings dined and danced, pampering themselves through spring. Finally, fearful of a surprise attack by Washington, whose troops were now rested, stronger and better trained, the British evacuated the city in June, taking with them most of Philadelphia's loyalist population.

Three more years of bloodshed followed until George Washington deceived the British in New York and trapped Cornwallis at Yorktown. Shortly thereafter, Benjamin Franklin, John Adams and John Jay signed a peace treaty with England.

The war may have ended but America entered what some historians have called the Critical Period, and others, the Lost Years. Millions of dollars in debt, the country had no authority to collect taxes, the best of families lost homes and farms to the depression, mobs terrorized certain parts of New England, and the rumor spread that soon the son of George III would reign as King in America.

At last, in 1787, a Constitutional Convention met in Philadelphia and began working on the country's problems. Initially the convention appeared ready to part in disagreement, but the members finally compromised, ratified a constitution, and the confederate states united as a nation. Later, the Electoral College unanimously elevated George Washington to the presidency.

The federal government had decided to make New York City its capital, but in late 1790 the legislators returned to Philadelphia to await completion of a new capital in Washington, D.C. For the next decade, the last of the 18th century, no city in America reigned more magnificently than Philadelphia.

People from everywhere continued moving into the City of Brotherly Love.

The proudest of all citizens were the Washingtons, who lived in a mansion at Sixth and Market Streets. A wall enclosed the first family's yard and orchard, but the Washingtons remained accessible to the people. Both President and Mrs. Washington entertained visitors almost daily, and the President, shy but warm, "liked to stroll about his capital in his black velvet smallclothes, visiting the markets, and saluting the citizens, and chatting with them occasionally," according to Struthers Burt.

All sorts of exciting events occurred in Philadelphia during these years, but the two most outstanding accomplishments of the period aroused little fanfare. John Fitch, a hard-luck, heavy-drinking fellow, experimented with steam power in 1786. The next year, he called several members of the Constitutional Convention to the banks of the Delaware and demonstrated a steam-powered boat. Later he placed a smoke-puffing, paddle-wheel steamer into the river for service between Philadelphia and Trenton. If only Fitch could have figured out how to keep his boats from blowing up, he might have then attracted a following. As it was, no one, including the President, placed much faith in steam power.

A young aeronaut, Jean Pierre Blanchard, fared a little better than Fitch when in 1793 he announced plans to stage America's first manned flight. The President, members of Congress, and about 1,000 other Philadelphians gathered at the corner of Sixth and Market Streets, behind Independence Hall, to debate Blanchard's chances of success. No one in Philadelphia had seen a man in flight before, so many people expected the 30-year-old Frenchman to fall to his death, if ever he got high enough off the ground. But Blanchard, who had piloted other balloons over Europe, knew exactly what he was doing. Before climbing into the basket that would carry him to an unknown destination, Blanchard accepted from the President a letter of introduction to the people who would presumably greet him upon landing. Then, all at once, Blanchard's huge, hydrogen-filled balloon lifted him off the ground, and as the crowd cheered, a westerly wind forced the balloon across the Delaware and into New Jersey. Ascending to 5,812 feet, Blanchard's flight lasted 46 minutes.

This happy, experimental mood continued in Philadelphia right through the turn of the century. Then the Golden Era abruptly ended, and with it died Philadelphia's prominence. The federal government moved to its permanent home. George Washington, John Adams, Thomas Jefferson, Benjamin Franklin —all were gone. Even the state government had moved on. Suddenly New York and Boston arose as the cities of importance in 19th century America. Philadelphia, now second to New York in population, remained comfortable and inviting, wealthy and promising, but never as interesting or as lively beyond the Golden Era.

# The City of Neighborhoods

Many a cynical observer has quipped that social Philadelphia fell asleep shortly after 1800 and only occasionally showed signs of life for the next century-and-a-half. In fairness, much continued to happen here, but the transformation from a cosmopolitan city to a provincial town did stick Philadelphia with a sleepy reputation.

However, visitors then, as now, rarely knew where to look for the *real* Philadelphia. They expected to find it in center city, that two-square-mile area of Penn's original boundaries where everything *always* happened, but an expanding center city left no space for visitors. By mid-century, Philadelphians had their heads buried in progress. They built street after street of rowhouses, narrow, yet two and three stories tall, for the city's half-million residents, and later they erected massive institutions and department stores, each building moving the city westward. For years this was the "Cradle of Finance," the money center of the nation, but commerce and credit excited bankers and capitalists and left others seeking something more stimulating. Still, anyone not part of Philadelphia's financial scene probably worked in manufacturing, and manufacturers made money, not glamour, so guests often felt disappointed in Philadelphia. Whatever it was that earlier travelers had found to rave about in the City of Brotherly Love, 19th century visitors said it had vanished.

Not so! Philadelphia had lost some of its glory, but Penn's town remained the richest and most culturally exciting city in the nation. Visitors, however, discovered Philadelphia only when they stumbled across the city's borders and into one of two dozen neighborhoods. There, in a friendly, stimulating environment, lived Philadelphia, and to this very day, the lifeblood of the city remains in its 110 ethnic neighborhoods. Native Philadelphians never say they're from Philadelphia. They're from Kensington, South Philly, Tacony, Harrowgate, Bella Vista, or some other neighborhood. Of which they are always proud.

Strangers who arrived in this new city — this New *World* — sought at least the comfort and security of living among people who spoke their language and shared their customs, and as immigrants entered Philadelphia, each nationality tended to claim its own community. This practice began in Penn's time and continued through the centuries, so that even today new neighborhoods are forming and old ones changing. Sometimes, one nationality moves to break ground elsewhere, and another nationality takes over. In other instances, the faces remain the same, but the neighborhood gets upgraded or it declines.

Most Philadelphia neighborhoods flourish. Each has its own identity, providing a main street, a shopping district, civic associations, a newspaper, a library, a moviehouse, health and medical services, and entertainment of various sorts, much of it centering around the neighborhood's ethnic cuisine. Public transportation serves all of the neighborhoods, connecting them with the city and with each other, but very few Philadelphians ever become intimate with more than one or two neighborhoods. People who live in South Philadelphia rarely have reason or desire to visit Northeast Philadelphia, and vice versa, and there is even less of a chance that residents in either place will travel to Manayunk (an Indian name meaning "where we drink") or Fishtown (so named by Charles Dickens in honor of England's fishing villages) or Juniata (another Indian name meaning "people of the standing rock"). It might be a good idea for neighbors to mingle across town, the way they do in the Midwest, but there is, after all, some truth to provincialism in Philadelphia. People here are oriented to home — they are not "street people" — and they are joiners. They belong to their private clubs (Philadelphia boasts more clubs than any city in America) and to their neighborhoods. In the security of their own environment, Philadelphians come alive.

Walk into South Philadelphia along the Ninth Street open-air market and suddenly you are in another world. Not far away stands Independence Hall, but people here are too emotional to notice, too busy selling mangoes, cheese, stuffed olives, zitis, breads, bracciolas, tomatoes, and a hundred other colorful, tasty foods. These Italians want everyone to feel at home, to eat, to buy, to laugh, but *not* to stay. If you don't speak the language it could be lonely living in South Philly, but not necessarily dangerous. South Philly is safe, and of Philadelphia's neighborhoods, this one ranks among everyone's favorite.

Italians were not the first to settle South Philly, one of the city's oldest neighborhoods. Several nationalities arrived earlier. Swedes and Finns were first, then blacks. By 1830 South Philly was a ghetto, the site of periodic race riots. The Irish arrived late in the century; then followed thousands of Eastern Europeans. As the blacks and Irish abandoned their homes for other parts of the city, Jewish and Italian immigrants moved in, and today, the Italians dominate the area. Around them live pockets of Irish, Jews, blacks, Poles and Slavs. Most of the residents are blue collar workers, though many are merchants in the famous Italian Market. They own immaculate rowhomes with polished picture windows, some displaying statues of the Blessed Virgin. During the summer months they sit in lawn chairs on their marble verandas from where they chat and shout, watching the teenagers on the corner, their sons, muscular and Fabian-like, some of them, their daughters, olive-skinned and pretty.

South Philly covers miles of territory and you could spend a lifetime here. Many people do. Beyond the market, several blocks long, there are schools and churches (the majority, Roman Catholic), night clubs and restaurants (Palumbo's the most famous), Veteran's Stadium, the Spectrum (for sports and entertainment), Franklin D. Roosevelt Park, the U.S. Navy Yard, Philadelphia International Airport, the Tinicum National Environment Center, and the Food Distribution Center, the world's first industrial park devoted exclusively to the food industry. How appropriate for South Philly!

In spite of the stay-at-home attitude that exists in South Philly (and in other neighborhoods) young people are always moving away. Unlike their parents, they want out of their village existence where they are surrounded by relatives and familiar places, so they spread into other neighborhoods and nearby New Jersey, too. Often they go in search of fame—Mario Lanza, Marian Anderson, Fabian, Joey Bishop, Frankie Avalon, Chubby Checker, Bobby Rydell, Connie Stevens, David Brenner, and others, all made it from South Philly.

There may be more talent in South Philly than in any other Philadelphia neighborhood, and each New Year's Day (weather permitting) some of that talent struts up Broad Street in a garish, comical Mummers' Parade, a Philadelphia exclusive. This infectious circus, which lures about a million people onto the blustery streets of Philadelphia, officially began in 1901, but the Mummers date to the earliest years of the city's history when youngsters reveled through the streets at Christmas time, shooting firecrackers and asking for penny donations.

In 1876, a group of Mummers (men only until recent years) paraded to Independence Hall in a half-march, half-dance strut, playing string instruments and dressed in gaudy costumes. Later the city organized the parade and awarded cash prizes. Since then, the Mummers compete on January 1, and in most Philadelphia neighborhoods at any given time of the year, someone is preparing for next year's parade, either practicing "Oh, dem Golden Slippers," the theme song, sewing costumes, or designing new routines for the bands. The Mummers present a spectacular show, now seen on national television, and the parade always begins from home—South Philly.

Across town from South Philly, in the northwest, lies the famous Philadelphia neighborhood of Germantown. Unlike the noisy Italian community, Germantown rests peacefully above the city, a refuge since its very earliest days.

Francis Daniel Pastorius obtained a charter from William Penn to settle Germantown in 1683 with a group of Dutch and German Quakers and Mennonites. Seeking religious freedom, they arrived aboard the ship, *America*. Earnest and home-loving (Philadelphia seems to attract homebodies) these people built log cabins along the Indian trail that eventually became Germantown Avenue, now a National Historical Landmark.

The Quakers and Mennonites, many of them devoted to arts, books and craftsmanship, signed America's first protest against slavery in 1688, and created a society apart from Philadelphia. Even though Germantown Road stretched into the city, six miles away, the settlers preferred to let the city folks come uphill to them. Since Germantown's higher altitude saved it from the unbearable heat and humidity of the city, and from the "fevers" that plagued Philadelphia, many wealthy citizens and some of America's most prominent families, favored this charming community during the summer months.

Strolling along Germantown Avenue today, visitors find a variety of houses and buildings reminiscent of by-gone America. For example, Wyck, the oldest house in Germantown, built in 1690 and occupied by the same family for nine generations through 1973 displays family portraits and personal possessions and invites tourists to roam about its two-acre lawn and rose garden. The Stenton Mansion, the plantation home of James Logan, Penn's secretary, served as headquarters for both Generals Washington and Howe during the American Revolution. Other homes open to the public include the Deshler-Morris House, where President Washington escaped Philadelphia's yellow fever epidemic in 1793; the Cliveden, a mid-Georgian country house built by Chief Justice Benjamin Chew; and Upsala, with its marble fireplaces and carved wooden cornices, an architectural treasure of the Federal period.

The names Pastorius, Washington and Logan are always associated with Germantown, but one nimble hausfrau who is rarely mentioned may have been the neighborhood's most courageous woman during the Revolution. Mom Rinker, as history has delivered her name, played a sly but decisive role in America's battle for independence. Sympathizing with the colonists, she secretly assisted the Green Boys, a local guerrilla group that battled the British and Hessian troops occupying Philadelphia. As the enemy moved in and out of the city along the Wissahickon Valley, Mom perched above them on a rock with her knitting, pretending not to notice their movement. Every so often she scribbled a message on paper, rolled it in a ball of yarn, and pitched the yarn 250 feet down the valley. Thanks to her help, the Green Boys mounted several surprising assaults, and Mom was Germantown's unknown heroine of the Revolution!

Long ago the Quakers and Mennonites left Germantown for the adjacent rich farmlands of Bucks and Montgomery Counties, but today their ideals are manifested by the many different nationalities that live in this successfully integrated, middle-class neighborhood.

There are other famous neighborhoods in Philadelphia, but even some of the least glamorous are favorites. Kensington, for example, is such a place. Unfortunately, only Kensingtonians seem to appreciate Kensington, famous for its white marble steps, many of them scrubbed daily for decades, and for Rocky Balboa, who feared becoming just "a bum from the neighborhood." No one ever visits Kensington *on purpose*, but when tourists lose their way between Old City Philadelphia and the greater Northeast, the moody ambience of this neighborhood overwhelms them. Kensington has been characterized as "a state of mind." Abounding with ruddy factories, old and small rowhouses, shabby taverns, narrow streets, brawny millworkers and others who work too hard for a living, Kensington tries to be a family community, but for most people the neighborhood is too rough and too parochial. Its residents are predominantly Irish Catholic and street smart — it has been said that Kensington's boys grow up to become priests, policemen or crooks — and racial incidents are endemic. However, homes are clean, neighbors and parents are respected, and Kensingtonians maintain a clanish pride. Other neighborhoods rival Kensington's milieu — Bridesburg, Tacony, Port Richmond, Shackamaxon, Brewery Town, and others that abut along the Delaware River — but Kensington remains one of a kind.

A different type of neighborhood exists across the Schuylkill River in west Philadelphia, which during the 19th century remained sparsely settled as the Welsh Barony, a country get-away for the city's upper class. Here the neighbors are usually black, with Irish, Italians, Slavs and Jews among them. University City, extending between 32nd and 40th Streets, encompasses Philadelphia's largest concentration of institutions, including the University of Pennsylvania, Drexel University, several hospitals, the Civic Center, the Commercial Museum, and University Museum. A diverse composite of races, ethnic groups, old residents, young families, students, professors and professionals creates a small college town atmosphere in Philadelphia.

Further west, the "Main Line" beckons affluent Philadelphia as it extends across three counties along the path of the old Pennsylvania Railroad. Haverford, Radnor, Merion, and Bryn Mawr are among the wealthiest communities in the nation. Their grand mansions and manicured gardens made the perfect setting for "The Philadelphia Story" with Katherine Hepburn.

In twentieth century America, however, no neighborhood in the country contains more history, more romance, more pleasure, than center city Philadelphia. It may have disappointed some visitors during parts of the 1800's and up through the first half of the 20th century, but changes have occurred since then, particularly since World War II, and now visitors frequently become so enamored with center city that they forget about exploring the other neighborhoods. Even W.C. Fields, who scoffed, "I went to Philadelphia one weekend and it was closed," would get a bang out of center city today.

The critical changes began during the late 1940's and they have continued through the present time. Politics, naturally, played a central role in everything that has happened. Republicans dominated both the state and city from the Civil War through the early 1950's, and City Hall's corrupt bureaucracy prevented social progress. But when the Democrats proposed Joseph S. Clark, Jr. for mayor on a sweeping platform of reform, the city flip-flopped politically, and it has remained a Democratic stronghold ever since. Clark, and succeeding mayors, charged the enthusiasm of the city's planners, and soon there seemed to be a bulldozer on every corner. In 1953, the massive Chinese Wall, an elevated masonry and steel railroad platform along Market Street, came tumbling down, signaling an expansive and costly urban renewal plan in the heart of Philadelphia.

Up to this time, the city's social life remained as tame as it had ever been in the 19th century. With a shortage of hotel space and few quality restaurants in Philadelphia, the convention trade and the big-spenders favored Atlantic City and New York. Indeed, Philadelphia remained the "City of Homes," where people watched television in the evenings and attended church on Sundays. Even home parties were not as lavish anymore, and the affluent society, squeezed by New Deal taxation, looked almost powerless at times.

Finally, life returned one day. Mayor Richardson Dilworth relaxed enforcement of the state's blue laws in the late fifties, and Philadelphians could do more on the weekends. Sunday sports enticed fans to the stadium, music concerts and shows opened in many neighborhoods, and eating out seemed like the natural thing to do. Suddenly the convention trade took a second look. Progress moved slowly, but everything happened in time for the nation's Bicentennial celebration. More than four million visitors arrived in town that year, and center city Philadelphia has yet to quit celebrating. Within a few years of America's 200th birthday party, more than 375 new eating emporiums opened in the city, offering cuisine from Poland, Greece, Thailand, Portugal—*everywhere*. The restaurant industry, with Le Bec Fin "the finest restaurant on the east coast," according to *Travel & Leisure* magazine, soon employed more people than any other sector of the city's economy. What a remarkable recovery for sleepy Philadelphia.

Happily, in spite of progress, the geography of Philadelphia has remained almost the way Penn planned it more than 300 years ago. The right-angle streets are curbed and paved now, but Penn would recognize them, that is if he could stop admiring his statue, 548 feet atop City Hall. From there he would certainly recognize his five squares:

Penn Square dominates the geographic center of town, and City Hall dominates Penn Square. Modeled after the Louvre in Paris, City Hall's construction required 29 years. Its blue slate and white marble texture, adorned with many pieces of sculpture, make this castle the city's most architecturally impressive sight. Completed in 1901, City Hall ranks among the largest municipal buildings in the world. Alexander Calder designed the bronze statue of Penn which faces northeast towards Penn Treaty Park, where the founding father supposedly negotiated his agreement of sale with the Indians. In deference to Penn, no building in Philadelphia surpasses the height of his statue, affording tourists a panoramic view from City Hall's observation tower.

"Establishment" Philadelphia dwells in the vicinity of City Hall, and so does "honky-tonk" Philadelphia. Bank headquarters, major law firms, corporate offices, and the Union League, the country's first Republican Club, are within a block or two south of Penn Square, towards Walnut Street, but east and west of City Hall, along Market Street, gaudy neon lights advertise adult books, peep shows, pinball palaces, taverns and X-rated theatres.

Just north of Market Street, steam engines used to belch into center city along the Chinese Wall, but tall office complexes now occupy that space, providing the "canyon" effect of downtown New York City.

A major modification of Penn's checkerboard layout occurred in the early 1900's when the city commissioned several architects, among them French landscape designer Jacques Greber, to design the Benjamin Franklin Parkway. This mile-long boulevard renders an uninterrupted vista from City Hall to the greenery of Fairmount Park at the Art Museum. In the style of the Champs Elysées, the Benjamin Franklin Parkway is a wide, tree- and flag-lined roadway, enriched by statues, three fountains, courtyards, gardens, the Rodin Museum, the Free Library, the Fels Planetarium, the Cathedral of Saints Peter and Paul, the Natural Science Museum, and the Franklin Institute. It ranks among the world's most culturally developed pieces of real estate.

As it cuts through one of Penn's original squares, the Benjamin Franklin Parkway creates Logan Circle (officially it's still Logan Square). In the 18th and 19th centuries, Logan Square served as pasture, burial ground and execution site, but in its present state the property serves no purpose save for beauty. Flower gardens surround a jetting fountain in the center of Logan Circle. Here, Pope John Paul II celebrated the Eucharist when he visited Philadelphia.

Six blocks south of Logan Circle, along 18th Street, Rittenhouse Square invites strollers and joggers to cross its path. Named after the astronomer David Rittenhouse, this square has witnessed some of Philadelphia's most elegant living. The townhouses bordering the square, particularly the one owned by Mrs. Sarah Drexel Fell Van Rensselaer, at 1801 Walnut Street, inspired the social scene in the early 20th century. Most of the old mansions have been razed, but several now house specialized institutions, such as the Penn Athletic Club, the Rittenhouse Club, the Curtis Institute and the Art Alliance. Today, Rittenhouse Square is one of the most popular parks in the city. It has become a meeting place for artists, musicians, business people, travelers, and smartly dressed Philadelphia matrons.

Washington Square attracts visitors eleven blocks east of Rittenhouse Square, not far from Independence Hall. It is the western boundary of Old City Philadelphia, beginning at Sixth and Walnut Streets. In the late 18th century residents used Washington Square for a potter's field, and in it rests the Tomb of the Unknown Soldier of the Revolutionary War. Consequently, patriotic celebrations frequently occur here, attended by tourists and residents from nearby apartment houses. The square was named for George Washington on the centennial of his birth.

Even in 1800 Washington Square sat too far west for residential development, so the neighborhood turned institutional and commercial. The first brownstone in the area belonged to the Athenaeum, Benjamin Franklin's private library club, and subsequently an active publishing trade followed. J.B. Lippincott Company occupied space around the square, as did the Curtis Publishing Company, then the publisher of *Saturday Evening Post* and *Ladies Home Journal*. The giant publishers have moved or disappeared, but a couple of smaller firms remain, including Lea & Febiger, America's oldest publishing company. Jeweler's Row developed a block away and the Walnut Street Theatre opened nearby. (The restored theatre is the oldest in continuous use in the English-speaking world). Nowadays, Washington Square makes an excellent starting point for walking tours of Old City Philadelphia.

The last of Penn's squares begins seven blocks north of Washington Square, on Race Street between Sixth and Seventh Streets. Unfortunately, the square's location, sandwiched between busy streets, Metropolitan Hospital and the Police Administration Bulding, leaves it an almost forgotten park. Ironically, this square was named for Benjamin Franklin, the city's most popular figure, but hardly anyone has reason to use Franklin Square, and a surprising number of Philadelphians would have no idea where to find it.

A block east of Franklin and Washington Squares begins "the most historic square mile in America." This is Independence National Historical Park.

Shamefully, by 1940 Old City Philadelphia had deteriorated to a slum, with many of its famous buildings an eyesore. But when the federal government declared the area a national historical park, the National Park Service implemented a major restoration. Wrecking crews demolished more than 200 decayed buildings, saving the most historic structures for restoration. Carpenters' Hall, the First and Second Banks of the United States, the home of Dolly

Madison, the Bishop-White House, Franklin Court, Betsy Ross' House, the American Philosophical Society, the Maritime Museum, Christ Church, Library Hall, Old City Hall, Congress Hall, and of course, Independence Hall—these and other sights recreate the colonial era in Philadelphia.

Many tourists need two or three days just to walk through Independence Park, following the paths of Franklin, Adams, Jefferson, *et al*. It is not unusual for people to lose themselves in time as they stand before Christ Church or sit in one of the colonial graveyards. History haunts every cobblestone and crack in America's most famous neighborhood, surprising even people who think they have no interest in the past.

As visitors explore Old City Philadelphia, they eventually stroll into Society Hill, a recently renovated affluent neighborhood, where history buffs hope to live forever. Of all their neighborhoods, Philadelphians are proudest of Society Hill, virtually a slum until 1950 when the city initiated its rebirth.

During Philadelphia's first 150 years, the stone streets of Society Hill supported the residential district, plus banking and commerce, but as the city moved westward, the residents followed. Society Hill became the warehouse division of Philadelphia.

Concurrent with the federal renovations in Independence Park, the city began one of America's most costly urban renewal projects in Society Hill, a name borrowed from the Free Society of Traders, a British stock company organized by Penn, and granted land at the foot of Pine Street, near the Delaware River. The Philadelphia Historical Commission surveyed significant historic landmarks in the neighborhood, and marked others for demolition. The city then purchased the residential structures and offered them for private, accurate restorations. New townhouses, most in contemporary designs, went up on the cleared lots, and young to middle-aged professionals moved into Society Hill. They have produced a quiet, refined community, more attractive than any other neighborhood in Philadelphia.

Alongside some of the most luxurious homes in America, Society Hill upholds several venerable but active churches, including a couple that date to the American Revolution. Head House Square, an early market and firehouse at Second and Pine Streets, is another attraction. The Head House has been restored and across from it developers have added New Market, a mall of quaint shops and restaurants. Adjacent to Society Hill is the less exclusive residential area, Southwark, a neighborhood pre-dating Penn. Merchants, captains and shipwrights settled with the Swedes in this river bank village, establishing the cynosure of shipbuilding in Philadelphia by the mid-18th century. (Of course, Philadelphia maintained the largest port in the New World.)

Penn's Landing, a waterfront recreation and educational park across from Society Hill, logically concludes a visit to Old City Philadelphia. It is here that people pause to remember William Penn, the Lord Proprietor, who struggled to bring forth Philadelphia, only to receive from it "trouble and poverty." The dream he carried to this shore has not vanished altogether. Faith has not overcome the world in Philadelphia, and no one mentions the "Holy Experiment" anymore, but Penn's prayer for his city has been answered. "O that thou mayest be kept from the evil that would overwhelm thee," Penn prayed, "that faithful to the God of thy mercies, in the life of righteousness, thou mayest be preserved to the end."

Philadelphia's destiny remains on course through its neighborhoods and people, and along with the rest of us, Penn would appreciate Philadelphia's style.

# THE PLATES

PENN'S LANDING


The Delaware River waterfront along Old City Philadelphia was once an eyesore and an embarrassment, but now the nautical mile between the Benjamin Franklin Bridge and Catharine Street is Penn's Landing, a popular site for residents and tourists. Presumably, William Penn landed here in October 1682.

Along with most of Old City Philadelphia, the waterfront became a warehouse district, and no one seemed to remember its historical significance. Then, in the 1960's, city developers dreamed of a romantic rebirth for the riverfront, and dramatic changes have occurred since then. Most of the warehouses are gone, and today Penn's Landing is a thriving center for education and recreation. Music, fireworks, stage plays and concerts are among the frequent attractions, and year-round displays include the Moshulu Maritime Exhibit, the largest steel sailing ship in the world, the *U.S.S. Olympia*, Commodore Dewey's flagship during the Spanish-American War, *the U.S.S Becuna*, a World War II submarine which also served in the Korean and Vietnam conflicts, the *Barnegat*, an iron lightship built in 1904, and *Gazela Primeiro*, a three-masted 178-foot barkentine built in Cachilhas, Portugal and launched in 1883. Restaurants and shops (New Market is just across the street) attract many visitors to the area.

The "Parade of Sail," tall ships from more than a dozen countries, docked at Penn's Landing in 1982 during Philadelphia's 300th birthday celebration.

# CHRIST CHURCH

The first landmark sighted by incoming ships to early Philadelphia must have been the 200-foot steeple above Christ Church. The present building, in the northwest corner of Second and Market Streets, was erected between 1727 and 1754, but a smaller Christ Church had been organized in 1695 by Philadelphia's Anglican community.

The Quakers who ruled Philadelphia originally denied a parish to the "Churchmen," but Penn had intended his land for all who prized religious freedom, and the Anglicans gradually increased in numbers. They built one of the best examples of colonial Georgian architecture in the city, and even non-worshippers admired the Palladian window on the Second Street façade. The communion table was made by Jonathan Gostelowe, a famous cabinet-maker, in 1788. The chandelier, brought from England in 1744, is still used today. The ring of eight bells, later increased to eleven, was cast in England and hung in the steeple in 1754. A wine glass shaped pulpit, used for 57 years by Bishop White, is one of the few original pulpits of its kind today.

Fifteen signers of the Declaration of Independence, and many prominent members of the community, worshipped at Christ Church. Seven of the signers, including Benjamin Franklin, were buried in the churchyard or in the cemetery at Fifth and Arch Streets. The Second Continental Congress worshipped at Christ Church in 1775 and 1776, and in 1790, pews 56 and 58 were reserved for President George Washington and his family. Behind them worshipped members of the Penn family, no longer Quakers.

The Protestant Episcopal Church was formed in Christ Church after the Revolution, and the National Shrine is an active parish today.

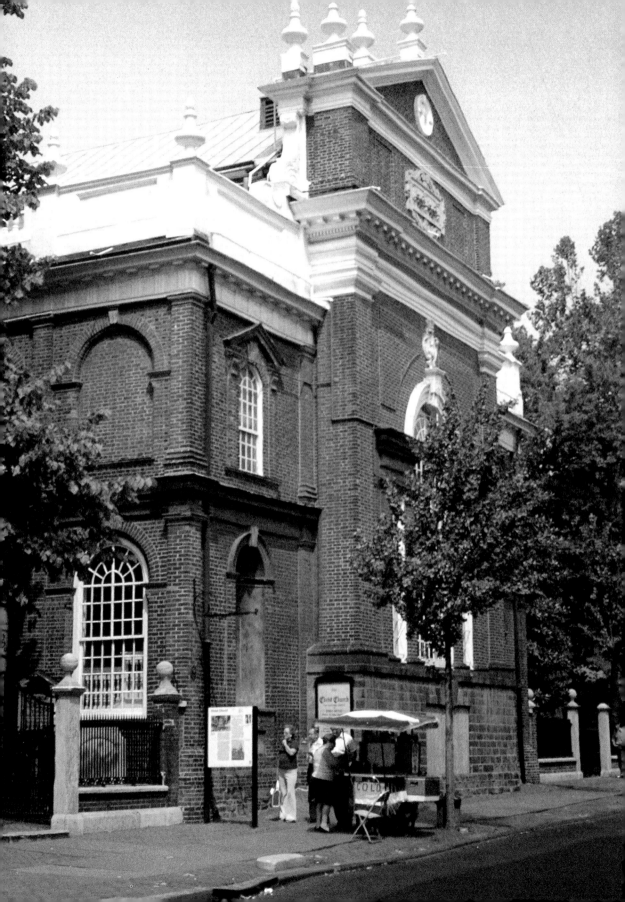

## SOCIETY HILL

Not so many years ago the street in this photograph cut through Philadelphia's worst commerical slum. Dilapidated buildings surrounded a polluting Dock Street Market, and traffic snarled on every corner. An entire home rented for $50 a month!

Late in the 1950's the Old Philadelphia Development Corporation decided to restore the deteriorated neighborhood. Many buildings were demolished, making room for new townhouses, and the city purchased certain residential structures and offered them for private, accurate restorations. The shabby Dock Street Market was destroyed and re-located in South Philadelphia. In just a few years the slum became Society Hill, a prestigious neighborhood where 18th century homes have been restored at costs of $50,000 to $100,000 and up, and new homes begin at about $85,000.

Most of Society Hill's residents are white tenants. Typically, the homes are colonial on the outside, contemporary inside. The restored neighborhood was supposed to attract older couples, but young professionals with money have settled here. They provide a liberal, quaint environment, perfect for weekend street fairs and evening strolls. Restaurants, shops and entertainment abound.

Society Hill was originally a tract sold by William Penn to the Free Society of Traders. Today, it is one of America's most successful urban renewal projects.

## BENJAMIN FRANKLIN BRIDGE

The Benjamin Franklin Bridge, originally the Delaware River Bridge, is one of the few assets from America's Sesqui-Centennial celebration in Philadelphia. Greedy Philadelphia politicians and businessmen bungled a grand birthday party proposed by merchant John Wanamaker.

The city created an international fair in the muddy flats of South Philadelphia because a few businessmen forced the selection of the inadequate site. The mayor opened the fair prematurely so that he could welcome his fellow Shriners. Few exhibits were ready and all but the main throughways remained unpaved so when it rained the fair turned to a mudhole. The Shriners went away unhappy and paid admissions only amounted to 6,408,829 persons, fewer than had visited Philadelphia's Centennial celebration. The outstanding exhibit was the Women's Committee re-creation of a colonial village. A huge deficit had to be assumed by the city's treasury.

The one gem from the international fair is the Benjamin Franklin Bridge, built in 1925, a masterpiece by engineer Ralph Modjeski. In South Philadelphia, seldom-used JFK Stadium, Municipal Stadium when it was built, is a white elephant reminder of the Sesqui-Centennial.

## NEW MARKET

In the mid-18th century, Philadelphians decided to build a second market-place along the Delaware River and several blocks below the original marketplace on High Street, now Market Street. They called the area New Market and the town's leading entrepreneurs provided land to build a community of homes in the neighborhood. A Head House served as a fire station, and behind it merchants opened stalls on Second Street at Lombard.

Most of the early buildings have been destroyed, but New Market was re-built during the urban renewal of Society Hill, Philadelphia's most prestigious neighborhood. Once again the area is a center for trade, residences and social life. The Head House and open air stalls remain, and as this photograph shows, a modern shopping/office complex has been added.

## CITY TAVERN

Colonial merchants and politicians frequently conducted business at the Blue Anchor Tavern, A Man Full of Trouble Tavern, and City Tavern, the "most genial one in America," according to John Adams.

Built by subscription in 1774, City Tavern offered lodging, spirits, coffee, taxed tea, Brunswick stew, bean soup and warm ale. Due to its location near the State House (Independence Hall), City Tavern was the most popular of Philadelphia's watering holes. Not only were commerce, trade and legal procedures debated here, but the tavern's walls also protected the plans of American revolutionaries. Military skirmishes were celebrated in the tavern throughout the War for Independence.

After 80 years of service, the tavern was demolished, but as part of the renewal in Independence Historical Park, City Tavern has been raised at Second Street between Chestnut and Walnut. Our photograph shows a view of the back porch.

## ELFRETH'S ALLEY

Elfreth's Alley is one of the few residential streets in North America where people have lived continuously since the 18th century. Rich and poor alike built homes along Elfreth's Alley, located between Front and Second Streets and Arch and Race Streets in Old City Philadelphia.

Originally it was Gilbert's Alley, named for the merchant John Gilbert, but Gilbert's son-in-law, Henry Elfreth, later named the alley for himself. The two- and three-story brick rowhouses were constructed during the early 1700's. Dwelling houses were added at the rear of the street-front homes, and residents approached them through narrow, arched passageways opening from the sidewalk. Water was supplied to the homes from pumps in the backyards.

Elfreth's Alley
an 18th Century Street
These homes continue to be
privately owned & occupied.
The public is invited to visit
Bladens Court and the
Museum House No 126
Please respect our privacy

## THE BETSY ROSS HOUSE

No one is certain Betsy Ross lived here or that she made the first flag here, but the Betsy Ross House at 239 Arch Street, just a few blocks from Independence Hall, contains many of Betsy Ross' personal possessions and portrays her life as flag-maker, upholsterer and patriot.

Betsy Ross lost two husbands in the Revolutionary War before she married John Claypoole, with whom she is buried in the Atwater Kent Park adjacent to her home. As a patriot, Betsy made flags for the Pennsylvania Navy, and, even though she was a Quaker, she made musket balls for the Continental Army. Betsy was also an upholsterer for Benjamin Franklin, the Society of Free Quakers, and the State House of Pennsylvania.

In their restored conditions, Betsy Ross' upholstery shop and home display work and family life in the 18th century. Among the furnishings which belonged to Betsy Ross are a highboy, chairs, spectacles, a snuff box and the Claypoole family Bible. This historic Philadelphia home has been furnished so that visitors may experience the life of a patriotic woman who contributed to America's heritage.

## CARPENTERS' HALL

Philadelphia's master carpenters formed the Carpenters' Company in 1742 as a labor union and as a society to help members develop architectural skills. In those days, craftsmen were designers as well as builders. The organization bought land on Chestnut Street and built Carpenters' Hall for its meeting place in 1770.

Four years later delegates of the First Continental Congress arrived in Philadelphia and convened at the City Tavern to choose a meeting place. They were offered the State House (Independence Hall) but they turned it down because of its conservative and royalist ties. They chose instead Carpenters' Hall. Here the delegates pondered the oppressive policies of an annoying British government. War was not a serious consideration, but at the conclusion of deliberations the Congress sent a petition for relief to King George III, then toasted him as the Royal Sovereign.

During the American Revolution Carpenters' Hall served as a hospital for both American and British forces, and the yard stored cannons and other war materials.

In 1857 the Carpenters' Company refurbished the building. Inside are nine Windsor chairs used by the First Continental Congress.

# THE GARDENS OF INDEPENDENCE

Independence National Historical Park, commemorating the events that established the United States as a free nation, includes 40 historic buildings on 42 acres of land. Certain buildings, Independence Hall among them, are originals; others, like City Tavern, are reconstructions. The landscape settings throughout the park are not original. Crowded colonial structures left little room for landscaping, but the remaining historic buildings are now surrounded by 18th-century-type plantings.

In 1736 the Pennsylvania Assembly reserved the grounds behind their new State House (now Independence Hall) as "a public open green and walks forever." At the time, these grounds were uneven and covered by whortleberry bushes and other vegetation. In 1784, the wealthy Jamaican planter, Samuel Vaughan, assumed the task of designing and supervising the planting of a formal garden. He based his plan on the new "naturalistic" style of gardening and completed his work in three years. A visitor to Philadelphia described the city as "a fine display of rural fancy and elegance."

Since colonial times the State House Yard has undergone many changes. Samuel Vaughan's garden has not survived, but more than 120 different types of trees and shrubs are now found in Independence National Historical Park, and ground cover, flower beds, lawns and an 18th century vegetable garden add variety to the area.

Our photograph shows the 18th Century Garden on the north side of Walnut Street between 3rd and 4th Streets. No other location in the city provides such a unique landscape feature. Maintained by the Pennsylvania Horticultural Society, this English garden exhibits species of trees, shrubs and flowers typical of those grown in the city prior to 1800. The cupola in the background rests atop Carpenters' Hall.

## SECOND BANK OF THE UNITED STATES

Philadelphia might have remained the center of America's financial world had it not been for a power struggle between President Andrew Jackson and Nicholas Biddle, president of the Second Bank. Early in the 1830's, the Second Bank was one of the most important financial institutions in the world, but when Biddle's conservative ideas crossed Jackson's liberal policies, the President blocked the renewal of the bank's charter. New York City succeeded Philadelphia as the financial center.

The Second Bank building was erected between 1819 and 1824, an adaptation of the Parthenon in Athens. William Strickland, architect of the steeple above Independence Hall, designed the building. The Second Bank was fully restored in 1974 and is now a portrait gallery dedicated to the founders of the United States. Many of the portraits were painted by Charles Willson Peale who at one time displayed his work on the second floor of Independence Hall. The building also includes a collection of William Birch prints depicting Philadelphia about 1800. The National Park Service used some of these engravings to restore City Tavern, Independence Hall and other park buildings.

## INDEPENDENCE HALL

No building anywhere means more to Americans than Independence Hall. Intended to serve as Pennsylvania's State House, this building became the meeting place for the Second Continental Congress in 1775–76; the site for George Washington's appointment as Commander-in-Chief of the Continental Army; and the scene for the signing of the Declaration of Independence and the Articles of Confederation. Within half a century the State House had reserved its place in history as Independence Hall.

Delegates from the thirteen colonies met in the Assembly Room for the Second Continental Congress. The room displays the "rising sun" chair that George Washington used during the Constitutional Convention. The inkstand on the President's desk was used when the delegates signed the Declaration of Independence and the Constitution.

Across from the Assembly Room, members of the Supreme Court conducted business. As visitors see today, the bailiff kept order in the court using a tipstaff, a long wooden pole with a brass head. Shackles subdued dangerous criminals.

Independence Hall, on Chestnut Street between Fifth and Sixth Streets, has endured many alterations, but the original Georgian beauty has been restored. The East and West wings have been re-built, as has the cupola which housed the Liberty Bell through 1976.

## THE LIBERTY BELL

This symbol of freedom throughout the world arrived in Philadelphia in 1752 and cracked upon its first ring. Foundrymen recast the bell twice to achieve a satisfactory tone, and for years thereafter the bell hung in the towers of the Pennsylvania State House, later re-named Independence Hall, tolling the hour, calling the citizens to meetings, and announcing special events.

During the American Revolution the bell was removed for fear the British would destroy it upon their invasion of Philadelphia, but later the Liberty Bell was returned to the tower. However, the bell cracked irreparably in 1835 during the funeral procession of Chief Justice John Marshall.

"Proclaim Liberty throughout all the land, unto all the inhabitants thereof," reads the Liberty Bell's inscription. Even in silence the bell communicates its message. The crack reminds us that freedom was not a gift.

At midnight, January 1, 1976, the Liberty Bell was moved to its own glass-enclosed pavilion in the shadow of Independence Hall. There visitors view it 24 hours a day.

# THE GRAFF HOUSE

Two blocks from Independence Hall, Thomas Jefferson wrote the Declaration of Independence in a room that he rented from the bricklayer, Jacob Graff, Jr. The Graff House, at 7th and Market Streets, has been rebuilt and Jefferson's parlor and bedroom refurnished in the way that the young Virginian might have used them.

With 34,400 residents, colonial Philadelphia was a noisy town when the 33-year-old Jefferson arrived to serve as a delegate in the Second Continental Congress, the War Congress. Although he was a popular man, Jefferson liked to spend his time alone, and so he rented rooms on the peaceful outskirts of town.

When the Congress entertained the idea of war with England, Jefferson was asked to draft a Declaration of Independence. He preferred to have Benjamin Franklin or John Adams write the document, but they persuaded him to create the first draft. As one who had studied the earliest human societies, and as a man concerned about justice and freedom, Jefferson was an excellent choice.

Notes from Jefferson's personal journal indicate that he bought gifts for his wife and strings for his violin in between writing sessions on a lap desk in the parlor. Every morning before he began work he soaked his feet in cold water to ward off colds. When the document was completed, Jefferson delivered it to his committee, and then to the Congress. After some debate, the Declaration of Independence was accepted on July 4, 1776. The only major change was the deletion of a clause renouncing slavery.

## THE ITALIAN MARKET

"Whaddaya' wanna buy?" You can buy almost everything in South Phi-ladelphia's Italian Market, a stretch of stalls and stores bulging with food, clothing, odds 'n ends, and mobs of people. Open daily except Sundays, there's no place more exciting for one-stop shopping.

Up and down Ninth Street hawkers push their merchandise and savvy shoppers compare the bargain prices. Most merchants sell produce in a brisk, take-it-while-it's-here manner. Don't dare pinch the tomatos, but don't hesitate to ask for a sample of cheese, olive mix or Italian salad. You'll also find homemade pastas, pastries, hard-crusted breads, live chickens, turkeys, lambs and goats, boned pig, artichokes, hard salamis, wine presses, garlic presses and macchinettas (for brewing Italian coffee). You can even buy scouring pads, toilet paper, window cleaner—all by the box—dresses, suits, ties, hats, and toys.

Cleanliness is *not* next to Godliness, but "'ey, *who* cares?"

# FOOD DISTRIBUTION CENTER

Fresh fish and produce have always been plentiful in Philadelphia. When the first of William Penn's followers arrived to build a town, they established an open air market on High Street, now Market Street. Gradually the town's food center expanded around Dock Street. But after years of use the market section deteriorated. In the modern city, open air stalls contributed to the pollution and congestion that frequently sent residents to the suburbs.

Eventually city agencies planned the demolition of the Dock Street Market and merchants were provided a new Food Distribution Center, the world's first industrial park devoted exclusively to the food industry. Built on a dump in South Philadelphia, it cost $4.5 million.

About fifty firms sell fruit and vegetables and another twenty sell seafood from the wholesale docks today. The center, covering more than 380 acres, also includes processing, packaging, freezing and warehouse facilities.

## PENNY FRANKLIN

Philadelphia school children collected 80,000 pennies, each with a fire prevention wish, to honor the 100th anniversary of Philadelphia's paid fire department. A Germantown sculptor, Reginald E. Beauchamp, then mounted the pennies on a bust of Benjamin Franklin, Philadelphia's most illustrious 18th century citizen and the author of *Poor Richard's Almanack*. Franklin was a printer, inventor, writer, statesman and businessman. He was responsible for many "firsts" in Philadelphia. Among his most important accomplishments were experiments with electricity, the invention of the Franklin stove, and the establishment of the Library Company. He also organized the Union Fire Company in 1736, the world's first volunteer group.

Penny Franklin was unveiled in June, 1971 at 4th and Arch Streets next to a fire house. In the background of the bust, artist Charles Santore has created "Portrait of a Patriot." Down the street from the bust the remains of Benjamin and Deborah Franklin rest in Christ Church Burial Ground. Across from the bust is the Arch Street Meeting House. Also close by is the home of Betsy Ross.

## CITY HALL

"Do we not say 'dear, dear Philadelphia' when we leave behind us this noble building to say it for us?" asked the orator at the cornerstone laying for City Hall in 1874.

Night or day, Philadelphia's City Hall is an eye-catching sight. Unitl 1908 it was the tallest building in America and for many years it remained the country's largest public building. Covering four-and-a-half acres, City Hall is larger than the United States Capitol and cost more than $24,000,000 to construct at the end of the 19th century.

City Hall's architectural style is French Renaissance. Built of granite and brick faced with marble, the building supports a 548-foot tower constructed of cast iron and plated with aluminum to look like stone. A bronzed William Penn graces the tip of the tower. Below the statue visitors may view the city from a breezy observation gallery, 480 feet above street level. Looking east there's Independence Hall and Old City Philadelphia with the Port of Philadelphia on the Delaware River and New Jersey just beyond. To the South, Broad Street leads to the stadium complex and Philadelphia International Airport. The northwest view seems to be everyone's favorite: Kennedy Plaza, Logan Square, the Benjamin Franklin Parkway, the Philadelphia Museum of Art—Philadephia's boulevard of culture. Due north, Broad Street runs to the suburbs, passing Temple University.

City Hall's 600 rooms house offices for the Mayor, the City Council, the Courts, and other administrative officials.

## THE MUMMERS

Never plan to drive in Philadelphia on January 1, because on that date 20,000 musicians, dancers and clowns own the city. They are the Mummers, and they attract up to one million spectators for a wild, day-long parade, weather permitting.

Mummering is as old as Philadelphia. At Christmas time, youngsters used to celebrate in the streets, shooting firecrackers and ringing doorbells to ask for penny donations. Through the years neighborhood musicians and clowns, males only until recent years, formed their own Mummers' groups, and in the early 1900's the city organized an annual Mummers' parade. Each New Year's Day more than two dozen string bands, playing the theme song, "Oh, dem Golden Slippers," and thousands of colorful clowns and "fancies" dance up Broad Street for $300,000 in prize money. Save for the Mardi Gras, there is no other comparable event in America.

Each Mummer makes a serious commitment to the parade, and in multi-generation Mummer families a son could be disowned for not participating. Planning for the day requires twelve months of work. Weekly practice sessions are mandatory for the musicians who learn new routines and music, and the clowns and "fancies" create different themes and formations. Most of the Mummers don elaborate costumes, like those shown in our photograph. One costume, including framework, feathers, sequins, mirrors, jewels, etc., may cost several thousand dollars for materials alone. Anyone who can thread a needle attends regular work sessions to build the costumes.

By the way, the Mummers rarely march, they strut or "cake walk," and you have to see this street dance before you can do it. Native Philadelphians are expert strutters. As they flap their arms like wings, they bow their heads, point their derrieres, and dance backwards. It may not sound graceful, but the look is rhythmical and funny, and uniquely Philadelphia.

68

# BENJAMIN FRANKLIN PARKWAY

William Penn laid out Philadelphia's streets in a checker-board pattern, but in 1910 the Fairmount Park Association engaged French landscape designer Jacques Greber to plan a diagonal parkway that would disrupt the monotony of the right-angle streets. Construction of the parkway did not begin until 1917. Upon completion it provided an uninterrupted vista from City Hall tower to the Art Museum at Faire Mount, as the hill at the western end of the city was then called.

The Benjamin Franklin Parkway was modeled after the Champs Elysées with statues, fountains and buildings set far back from wide roads lined by trees and flags. Logan Square, surrounded by cultural and religious institutions (including the Franklin Institute and the Cathedral of Saints Peter and Paul), is approximately the mid-way point of the mile-long boulevard, shown in this photograph. The fountain in the foreground of our photograph is in John F. Kennedy Plaza, and the circular building to the left is the Philadelphia Convention and Visitors Bureau.

# LOGAN SQUARE

William Penn instructed the architects of his "Holy Experiment" — Philadelphia — to lay out a "greene countrie towne," with spacious lots for homebuilders and five public squares. Most of the spacious lots have disappeared — row-houses became a necessity — but the five public squares have remained. City Hall occupies Penn Square in the center of Philadelphia, and in the quadrants, Logan, Rittenhouse, Washington and Franklin Squares are colorful, open parks. Rittenhouse is the most famous of the five; Franklin the least used. Our photograph shows Logan Square (also called Logan Circle), at one time a burial ground, pasture and execution site. In 1825 the square was named for James Logan, Penn's secretary, and the Chief Justice of Pennsylvania.

Construction of the Benjamin Franklin Parkway in the early 20th century modified Logan Square by rounding off its corners. Around the circle some of Philadelphia's most important cultural buildings have been erected, representing French, Roman-Corinthian, Greek and Victorian architecture. The Rodin Museum, the Cathedral of Saints Peter and Paul, the Academy of Natural Sciences, the Free Library, Philadelphia County Courthouse, the Franklin Institute and the Moore College of Art are all within a block of Logan Square.

In 1924, sculptor Alexander Stirling Calder created the three heroic figures holding swans and fish in the fountain at Logan Square. The nudity of the figures created a furor in Philadelphia. Calder explained that the statues symbolize the city's three bodies of water: the man, the Delaware; the mature woman, the Schuylkill; the young woman, the Wissahickon. Now everyone overlooks the nudity, and regardless of the season, Logan Square is a pleasant scene. When Pope John Paul II visited the United States, he celebrated the Eucharist at Logan Square.

# THE PHILADELPHIA MUSEUM OF ART

Rising above the Benjamin Franklin Parkway at the entrance to Fairmount Park, the Philadelphia Museum of Art sprawls across ten acres of land. The museum marked its centennial in 1976 as one of the great art institutions of the world.

With funds provided by the city, the Fairmount Park Commission authorized construction of the museum in 1919. An earlier art gallery had been constructed for the Centennial Exposition of 1876. Today's impressive Greco-Roman museum houses more than 500,000 works of art.

Containing more than 200 galleries, the museum traces the history of art through the centuries in different countries, with works of painting, sculpture, furniture, ceramics and other arts. The South Wing is devoted to the art of Asia from Japan to China, India and Iran. The North Wing displays the art of continental Europe from the Renaissance to modern times.

Among the museum's most prized exhibits are the Oriental collections; the Johnson collection of 14th–19th century European painting; the Elkins collections of European and American masters; the Stern, Gallatin, Arensberg and Tyson collections of 19th and 20th century art; and the Geesey collection of Pennsylvania German arts. The museum administers the Rodin Museum along the Benjamin Franklin Parkway, and the exhibits of American art in several colonial homes throughout Fairmount Park.

The steps leading to the museum are almost as famous as the museum itself, for on these steps Rocky Balboa (Sylvester Stallone) trained for his fight in the motion picture, *Rocky*.

74

# PHILADELPHIA SCULPTURE

A city with a cracked Liberty Bell ought to also have a crooked O in the word love, and thus is the case in Philadelphia. Robert Indiana's LOVE stands among more than 450 pieces of public sculpture, a record number for American cities. By law, one percent of every construction contract within Philadelphia goes into a fund for the "aesthetic ornamentation of city structures," a practice that other cites are now adopting.

William Rush's "Water Numph and Bittern" (1799) was the city's first decorative sculpture built with public funds. In 1872, the Fairmount Park Art Association decided to "promote and foster the beautiful in the city of Philadelphia, in its architecture, improvements and general plan" and embellished the park with sculpture. The idea spread throughout the city.

Some of Philadelphia's most famous public art includes: Louis Barye's, "Lion Crushing A Serpent;" Jonn J. Boyle's, "Stone Age in America;" Frederic Remington's, "Cowboy;" Alexander Stirling Calder's "Swann Memorial Fountain;" Joseph Brown's social realist depiction of "Benjamin Franklin, Craftsman;" and Claes Oldenburg's, "Clothespin," the most notorious ("I'll meet you at the Clothespin," Philadelphians say) and controversial ("*What* does it mean?") of the city's sculpture.

For visitors, the Institute of Contemporary Art has published Urban Encounters, a free walking tour map of public art in Philadelphia.

76

## THE MANSIONS OF FAIRMOUNT PARK

The largest landscaped park system within city limits in the world is Fairmount Park in Philadelphia. More than 8,000 acres await Philadelphians and tourists for year-round entertainment, recreation and education.

Within the boundaries of Fairmount Park are the Philadelphia Museum of Art, the Philadelphia zoo, Playhouse in the Park, the Robin Hood Dell, an outdoor amphitheatre showcasing a "Summer Festival of Stars," Boathouse Row, dozens of statues and sculpture, and the Schuylkill waterfront for sculling and sailing.

Fortunate are those who discover the best treasures of Fairmount Park — the several mansions hidden in the sylvan hills above the Schuylkill Valley. These historic homes reveal architectural Philadelphia during the Golden Era, the years between 1720 and 1800.

In our photograph is Strawberry Mansion dating from 1797 and built by jurist William Lewis in the Federal style. The home was called Summerville until the mid-19th century and among its guests were President George Washington and Secretary of the Treasury Alexander Hamilton. Judge Joseph Hemphill bought the home to enhance his political position in the 1820's and his two spoiled sons nearly destroyed the place. Son Coleman built a race track, raised Dalmatians and imported strawberry roots from Chile. Son Alexander recklessly built a south wing to do some sport entertaining. Later, a north wing was added to restore the mansion's balance.

Horrible as it sounds, Strawberry Mansion became a roadhouse selling strawberries and cream. Finally the Park Commission acquired the building in 1869 and began a complete restoration. The trolley out front is used to carry tourists throughout the park and city. Other mansions in the park include Lemon Hill, named for its hothouse lemon trees and Mount Pleasant, a Georgian Mansion once owned by Benedict Arnold.

## OLD PHILADELPHIA WATERWORKS

From across the Schuylkill River, the Philadelphia Museum of Art towers above the Old Philadelphia Waterworks where Fairmount Park begins. Engineering genius Frederick Graff developed the waterworks, the largest on the continent at the time, and made tap water so plentiful that Philadelphians used it to scrub their steps and sidewalks, much to the amazement of visitors.

On spring and summer evenings during the 19th century, it was an adventure for smartly dressed gentlemen to bring their ladies to the east bank of the Schuylkill for a stroll along the waterworks' promenade. When Charles Dickens inspected the site he was much impressed. He said the waterworks were "no less ornamental than useful, being tastefully laid out as a public garden and kept in the best and neatest order."

While the waterworks are no longer used today, people still return to the area to see the Azalea Garden in the springtime, the Lincoln Monument, the Seashore Fountain (a gift: from Italy for Philadelphia's Sesqui-Centennial celebration) and the Riley Memorial of Revolutionary War statues. From the edge of the promenade visitors will find the best view of Boat-house Row along East River Drive.

# EAST RIVER DRIVE

No one who visits Philadelphia should miss East River Drive which hugs the Schuylkill River and bursts into color during the spring. When William Penn chose the peninsula that would become Philadelphia, he envisioned the importance of the Delaware River to the east, and the Schuylkill River to the west. The latter never achieved the commercial significance of the former, but for beauty and recreation, the Schuylkill River must have satisfied Penn's expectations.

The Schuylkill provides one of the world's straightest and widest rowing courses, and Philadelphia is a famous sculling center. Many Olympians and other world class oarsmen — Jack Kelly Sr. and Jr. among them — trained on the Schuylkill. A favorite view along the riverbank is created by Boathouse Row, a line of Victorian turreted boathouses. The homes were built after 1850 by private groups and are now occupied by nine rowing clubs. The clubs make up the Schuylkill Navy, the oldest amateur athletic governing body in America.

Visitors may rent canoes and rowboats at a public boathouse near the Strawberry Mansion Bridge.

## PHILADELPHIA ZOOLOGICAL GARDEN

As you might have guessed, Philadelphia sponsored America's first zoo. Today, the Philadelphia zoological Garden, at 34th and Girard in Fairmount Park, is internationally known for its artistic and naturalistic form of exhibits, plus its studies of animal diseases, birdly and beastly diet, and the longevity of its captives. Massa, the world's oldest captive gorilla, is one of Philadephia's most popular personalities.

The Civil War prevented Philadelphia from opening its zoo prior to July 1, 1874, but at that time forty-three species greeted the public. Since then, more than 500 species of mammals have been exhibited here. Visitors may roam about the park or ride the Safari Monorail which rolls through the treetops and above the animals. Recorded jungle sounds and a brief narrative make the excursion all the more exciting.

The zoo's Hummingbird Exhibit is one of its best. Brilliantly colored birds fly about in a climate-controlled Paradise, complete with vegetation and shiny waterfalls.

By the way, the lions eat at 3 p.m.!

## DESHLER-MORRIS HOUSE

In the late summer of 1793, when Philadelphia was the capital of America, yellow fever struck and put a "strange and melancholy ... mask on the once carefree face of a thriving city." Fortunately, Congress was not in session. The Supreme Court met for one day in August and quickly adjourned. The executive branch remained in town only through early September. "A contagious and mortal fever ... is driving us all away ..." wrote Thomas Jefferson, then Secretary of State.

President Washington moved to Mount Vernon but by late October decided to return to Philadelphia. For safety he rented this home in nearby, airy Germantown. Here, during November, Washington prepared for his fifth annual address before the Congress. The next summer he and his family returned to the home to spend several months in peaceful Germantown.

David Deshler, a Philadelphia Quaker merchant, built this handsome Georgian home on Germantown's Market Square in the 1750's. He used the home for two decades as his country residence, but after the Battle of Germantown in the autumn of 1777, British Commander Sir William Howe turned the home into his headquarters. Washington's troops badgered the enemy for two weeks until Howe finally ordered his tired army back to Philadelphia, leaving the home to the Deshler family.

Germantown was settled by Francis Daniel Pastorius and his Dutch and German followers who created a society apart from Philadelphia in 1683. Many historic homes and buildings have been restored for visitors in Germantown, which lies below wealthy Chestnut Hill.

## MAIN LINE PHILADELPHIA

"Among the quiet valleys west of Philadelphia lies one of the loveliest areas in the world, the Main Line." James A. Michener wrote those words for *Holiday* magazine in 1950. Today, the words ring true. Main Line Philadelphia represents suburban America at its best.

As Michener pointed out, the Main Line may not be the only residential area named for a freight track — the region straddles the tracks of the Pennsylvania Railroad — but here there is no wrong side of the tracks. The great names of Philadelphia society lived along the Main Line — the Cadwaladers, Cassatts, Chews, Biddles, Robertses and Drexels, and later the Wideners, the Dorrances, the Strawbridges and the Pews. The Golden Era of the Main Line struck between 1900 and 1929. In those days, Main Line families spent the winter in Florida, summered in Newport or Bar Harbor, and lived the remainder of the year in their palaces and in dwellings around Rittenhouse Square in Philadelphia.

All that has changed since the Depression. The Main Line remains wealthy, but Main Line families have become less formal and extravagant. Some of their mansions were demolished to cut taxes during the New Deal era, but many examples of the fine living remain. Appleford, photographed here with its formal twentieth century garden and sculpture, is a pleasant reminder of the good life. The L shaped mansion dates from 1705. Its last owner bequeathed the home to the citizens of the community.

88

## VALLEY FORGE

"These are the times that try men's souls. The summer soldier and the sunshine patriot will in this crisis, shrink from the service of his country; but he that stands it NOW, deserves the love and thanks of man and woman . . ." So began Thomas Paine, author of *Common Sense*. How Paine's words must have inspired General Washington's men as they camped that dreadful winter at Valley Forge.

"To see men without clothes to cover their nakedness, without blankets to lie upon, without shoes . . . without a house or hut to cover them until those could be built, and submitting without a murmur, is a proof of patience and obedience which, in my opinion, can scarcely be paralleled," wrote George Washington at Valley Forge, December 23, 1777.

Washington's army struggled into snow-covered Valley Forge on December 19. Tired, cold and ill-equipped, the men had little training for the battlefield, but after six months of encampment they emerged to meet the British army at the Battle of Monmouth in New Jersey.

More than three million people visit Valley Forge National Historical Park each year. There are 2,500 acres of parkland, and the encampment may be visited by tour bus, bicycle or private automobile. A Visitor's Center provides historical background and tour information.

## WASHINGTON CROSSING STATE PARK

Not far north of Philadelphia, in lush Bucks County, George Washington and his troops crossed the Delaware and surprised the Hessians at Trenton in 1776. After a string of defeats, the sudden victory lifted the spirits of a depressed army and Congress.

Washington had crossed the Hudson into New Jersey to join forces with General Greene, and they marched southward with General Cornwallis in pursuit. After several days the British gave up the chase and by mid-December retreated to winter quarters, leaving defense forces at Trenton and Princeton.

The British knew that Washington had crossed the Delaware going south, but the American General later deceived the enemy by turning north and *re-crossing* the Delaware during a stormy Christmas night. In two divisions and 2,400 soldiers strong, Washington's attack on Trenton came from two directions the morning of December 26. The Hessians had already celebrated Christmas; the American troops had a heartier celebration a day late.

Washington Crossing State Park is a lovely memorial along the banks of the Delaware River. A Memorial Building displays a copy of Emanuel Leutze's *Washington Crossing the Delaware* and a taped narration explains Washington's encampment on the river and the events leading to the moment captured in Leutze's painting. The Washington Crossing Library of the American Revolution is also in the building. Close by is the Old Ferry Inn where Washington ate dinner and waited with his staff to cross the river.

## PHILADELPHIA SKYLINE

"And thou Philadelphia, the virgin settlement of the province, named before thou wert born, what love, what care, what service, and what travail have there been to bring thee forth and preserve thee from such as would abuse and defile thee, O that thou mayest be kept from the evil that would overwhelm thee, that faithful to the God of thy mercies, in the life of righteousness, thou mayest be preserved to the end. My Soul prays to God for thee, that thou mayest stand in the day of trial. That thy children may be blest of the Lord. And thy people saved by His power."

William Penn's Prayer For Philadelphia, 1684

94